Yellow Umbrella Books are published by Capstone Press
151 Good Counsel Drive, P.O. Box 669, Mankato, Minnesota 56002
www.capstonepress.com

Library of Congress Cataloging-in-Publication Data
Endres, Hollie J.
   Push and pull / by Hollie J. Endres.
     p. cm.
     Summary: Photographs and easy-to-read text illustrate how various objects can be
moved by pushing or pulling them.
     ISBN 0-7368-2921-0 (hardcover)—ISBN 0-7368-2880-X (softcover)
     1. Force and energy—Juvenile literature. [1. Force and energy. 2. Mechanics.]
I. Title.
QC73.4.E53 2004
531'.6—dc21   2003008402

Editorial Credits
Editorial Director: Mary Lindeen
Editor: Jennifer VanVoorst
Photo Researcher: Wanda Winch
Developer: Raindrop Publishing

Photo Credits
Cover: BananaStock; Title Page: DigitalVision; Page 2: Royalty-Free/Corbis; Page 3:
Royalty-Free/Corbis; Page 4: Royalty-Free/Corbis; Page 5: Dave Lissy/Image Ideas,
Inc.; Page 6: Andersen-Ross/Brand X Pictures; Page 7: Ryan McVay/PhotoDisc; Page 8:
Craig Aurness/Corbis; Page 9: Royalty-Free/Corbis; Page 10: BananaStock; Page 11:
EyeWire; Page 12: Elyse Lewin/Brand X Pictures; Page 13: DigitalVision; Page 14:
Doug Menuez/PhotoDisc; Page 15: Royalty-Free/Corbis; Page 16: Comstock

Push and Pull

by Hollie J. Endres

Consultant: Paul Ohmann, PhD, Assistant Professor,
Department of Physics, University of St. Thomas

Yellow Umbrella Books

an imprint of Capstone Press
Mankato, Minnesota

How can you move an object from one place to another?

You can push it or you can pull it.
Both a push and a pull are a force.

Let's talk about the force of a push. You can use your body to push something away from you.

You can push a swing
to make it move.

What else can you push? You can push a broom to make it sweep.

You can push a cart
to make it roll.

What else can you push? You can push a door to make it shut.

8

Can you push a ball
to make it move?

Let's talk about the force of a pull. You can also use your body to pull something toward you.

You can pull a wagon
to make it move.

What else can you pull? You can pull a toy to make it move.

You can pull a sled
to make it slide.

What else can you pull? You
can pull a rope to make it move.

Can you pull on a sock?

What else can you push?
What else can you pull?

Words to Know/Index

Word Count: 184
Early-Intervention Level: 12